Beyond Band-Aids: A Holistic Approach to Child Safety and Accident Prevention

AUTHORS

Dr. Prasad L. Jaybhaye,
MBBS, MD, Forensic medicine

Dr. Minakshi Ghuge (Jaybhaye),
MBBS, MD, DCH

FROM THE AUTHORS DESK

I would like to express my heartfelt gratitude to the Almighty for inspiring me with the idea and opportunity to develop this innovative piece of literature. During my postgraduate studies, I encountered a profoundly impactful experience while conducting a post-mortem examination on a three-year-old child whose tragic passing resulted from scald injuries. This moment left an indelible mark on my memory and sparked a commitment to create something that would raise awareness among parents and children about their surroundings. This book serves as my tribute to all the innocent lives that could have been preserved through increased awareness.

While this book is primarily designed for readers aged five to fifteen years, its content is relevant for individuals of all ages seeking to enhance their understanding of safety and awareness. I believe this work has the potential to save millions of innocent lives worldwide. As an individual, my capacity to reach others is limited; however, if each reader makes a small effort to share this book with others, we can collectively effect significant change. It is my hope that this book will contribute to fostering peace for all.

Dr. Prasad L. Jaybhaye

Email: drprasadjaybhaye@gmail.com

This book is dedicated to
My parents, who taught me the importance of truth and benevolence.
Dr. C.S. Kapse Sir who taught me the importance of ethics.
Dr. Radhakrishnan Sir and Dr. Rex Thomas Sir from whom I learnt importance of humble attitude
Dr Swati Shiradkar madam from whom I learnt importance of patience
My teachers, Kankale Sir, Sapkal Sir, Nagore Sir, whose excellent teaching skills helped me in my education.
My sisters for their constant love and support.

अभयं सत्वसंशुद्धिर्ज्ञानयोगव्यवस्थिति: ।
दानं दमश्च यज्ञश्च स्वाध्यायस्तप आर्जवम् || 1||
अहिंसा सत्यमक्रोधस्त्याग: शान्तिरपैशुनम् ।
दया भूतेष्वलोलुप्त्वं मार्दवं ह्रीरचापलम् || 2||
तेज: क्षमा धृति: शौचमद्रोहोनातिमानिता ।
भवन्ति सम्पदं दैवीमभिजातस्य भारत || 3||

"these are the saintly virtues of those endowed with a divine nature—fearlessness, purity of mind, steadfastness in spiritual knowledge, charity, control of the senses, sacrifice, study of the sacred books, austerity, and straightforwardness; non-violence, truthfulness, absence of anger, renunciation, peacefulness, restraint from fault-finding, compassion toward all living beings, absence of covetousness, gentleness, modesty, and lack of fickleness; vigor, forgiveness, fortitude, cleanliness, bearing enmity toward none, and absence of vanity."

...**Bhagavad Gita: Chapter 16, Verse 1-3**

Table of contents

<u>**SECTION I**</u>

1. ACCIDENTAL INJURIES IN CHILDREN: A PUBLIC HEALTH PERSPECTIVE ON PREVENTION.

Accidental injuries are a serious threat to children globally, demanding comprehensive preventative measures and robust data collection for effective intervention. This review will explore the burden of accidental injuries in children, examining their prevalence across demographics, common causes, and the role of public health in mitigating risks.

Magnitude of the Problem: Unintentional Injuries and Their Impact [1,2]

Available data suggest that unintentional injuries constitute a major public health concern for children, impacting their health, well-being, and future prospects. Key insights from the previous research includes:

- **Global Disparities:** While unintentional injuries affect children worldwide, the burden is disproportionately higher in developing nations. This disparity is likely due to a combination of factors, including underdeveloped infrastructure, limited access to healthcare, and variations in safety standards.

- **Magnitude of the Problem:** In the United States, unintentional injuries rank as the primary cause of death among individuals aged 1 to 19, exceeding all other causes of death combined within this demographic. The studies highlight that even non-fatal injuries can lead to significant long-term effects, adversely affecting a child's development, educational opportunities, and overall quality of life.

- **Data Collection Challenges:** A critical challenge in tackling this issue is the lack of comprehensive and standardized data collection on childhood injuries, particularly in developing countries. Without reliable data, accurately assessing the full scope of the problem and designing targeted interventions becomes significantly harder.

''Future depends on what we do in the present''

2. Exploring the Epidemiology of Accidental Injuries in Children

Review of the data available from scientific literature [3] shed light on how accidental injuries disproportionately affect specific demographics, emphasizing the need for tailored interventions:

- **Age as a Key Determinant:** The risk of particular injuries correlates strongly with a child's age and developmental stage. For example, while suffocation in unsafe sleeping environments is a primary concern for infants under one year old, the risk decreases significantly in older age groups. Conversely, older children, with increased mobility and independence, become more vulnerable to road traffic accidents and drowning.

- **Boys at Higher Risk:** Data consistently reveals a higher rate of unintentional injury deaths in boys compared to girls. While the exact reasons for this discrepancy remain unclear, researchers suggest a potential link to biological factors, societal expectations, and risk-taking behaviors, which tend to be more prevalent among boys.

- **Socioeconomic Factors:** The sources indicate that children from lower socioeconomic backgrounds are disproportionately affected by unintentional injuries. This disparity likely stems from a complex interplay of factors, including limited access to safe housing, neighborhoods, and healthcare, as well as potential differences in parental supervision and awareness of safety measures.

''Tomorrow Will Be Beautiful''

3. Common Causes of Accidental Injuries in Children

Available data [2,4] highlights common causes of accidental injuries in children, providing insights into their mechanisms and associated risk factors:

1. Road Traffic Incidents (RTIs)

- **A Leading Cause of Death:** RTIs are a leading cause of accidental death for children globally, particularly among children older than one year. Rapid urbanization and increased motorization, especially in developing countries, contribute to the growing number of RTIs involving children.

- **Pedestrian Vulnerability:** A significant proportion of RTIs in children, particularly in low-income countries, involve pedestrians. This underscores the need for pedestrian-friendly infrastructure, traffic calming measures, and educational programs to promote safe road-crossing behaviours.

- **Role of Restraint Systems:** The use of age-appropriate restraint systems like car seats and booster seats has been shown to dramatically reduce the severity of injuries in children involved in RTIs. However, improper installation, incorrect usage, and non-compliance with car seat laws remain significant challenges, emphasizing the need for continued education and awareness campaigns.

2. Drowning

- **A Quiet Danger:** Drowning is a significant cause of mortality in young children, particularly those between the ages of 1 and 4. The swift and often unnoticed occurrence of drowning provides minimal opportunity for rescue, underscoring the critical importance of prevention measures.

- **Unsupervised Water Access:** The most significant risk factor for drowning is unsupervised access to water, be it swimming pools, bathtubs, or open water sources like ponds and lakes. Effective prevention strategies include installing barriers around pools, supervising children closely around water, and teaching them basic water safety skills from a young age.

- **Swimming Lessons:** Formal swimming lessons can provide children with essential skills and knowledge to stay safe in and around water. However, access to swimming lessons can be limited, particularly in low-income communities and developing countries, highlighting the need for affordable and accessible water safety programs.

3. Falls

- **Age-Related Risks:** Falls are a leading cause of nonfatal injury in children, with the type and severity of injuries varying significantly with age. Infants and toddlers are prone to falls from furniture, stairs, and playground equipment, while older children are at risk of falls from greater heights, such as trees, windows, and balconies.

- **Home Safety Measures:** Most falls occur at home, emphasizing the importance of childproofing measures to prevent falls, particularly for young children. Installing safety gates at the top and bottom of stairs, securing furniture to prevent tip-overs, and supervising young children closely, especially around windows and balconies, are critical preventative measures.

- **Playground Safety:** Playgrounds are another common location for falls, highlighting the need for regular inspection and maintenance of equipment, as well as the importance of soft surfacing to cushion falls. Additionally, educating children on safe playground behaviors, such as avoiding pushing and shoving, can help minimize the risk of falls.

4. Burns

- **Scald Injuries:** Burns, especially those caused by hot liquids, are a significant contributor to injuries and fatalities in young children. The kitchen is a common site for scald injuries, highlighting the need for safe cooking practices, such as turning pot handles inwards, and keeping hot liquids out of reach of children.

- **Water Heater Temperature:** Setting the temperature of the water heater to a maximum of 120°F (49°C) can greatly lower the likelihood of serious burns. Hot water at higher temperatures can cause third-degree burns in a matter of seconds, making this a simple yet crucial preventative measure.

- **Other Burn Types:** Contact burns from hot objects, such as irons and stoves, and electrical burns are also significant concerns. Teaching children about the dangers of hot surfaces and keeping electrical cords and appliances out of reach are essential preventative steps.

5. Poisoning

- **Developmental Vulnerability:** Young children, with their developing cognitive abilities and natural curiosity, are particularly vulnerable to accidental poisoning. They may mistake medications for candy or ingest household cleaners and chemicals due to their appealing colors and smells.

- **Safe Storage:** The cornerstone of poisoning prevention is the safe storage of medications, cleaning products, and other potentially hazardous substances. This includes keeping them in their original containers, out of sight and reach of children, and using child-resistant closures.

- **Poison Control Centers:** Knowing the national poison control number and having it readily accessible is crucial in case of accidental ingestion. Poison control centers provide expert advice and guidance on managing poison exposures, and immediate contact can be life-saving.

4. Public Health Interventions

A Multifaceted Approach to Prevention [1,2]:

- **Education and Awareness:** Educating parents, caregivers, and children about common injury risks and age-appropriate safety measures is paramount. Public awareness campaigns, community outreach programs, and **school-based education can play a significant role** in promoting safe behaviors and fostering a culture of safety. *(please see section 2 for school-based educational activities)*

- **Environmental Modification:** Creating safer environments for children is essential in preventing accidental injuries. This includes implementing safety measures in homes, schools, and public spaces, such as installing window guards, safety gates, and playground safety features. Additionally, improving road design, implementing traffic calming measures, and ensuring safe access to recreational areas are crucial aspects of environmental modification.

- **Legislation and Enforcement:** Enacting and enforcing legislation can effectively address key risk factors and contribute to a significant reduction in childhood injuries. Mandatory seat belt laws, regulations on the safety of playground equipment, and requirements for child-resistant packaging on medications and household products are all examples of effective legislative interventions.

5. Conclusion: A Shared Responsibility to Protect Children

Accidental injuries in children are preventable tragedies with potentially devastating consequences. Addressing this global public health issue demands a collective effort involving parents, caregivers, healthcare providers, policymakers, education system and communities as a whole.

References:

1.ADVANCING CHILD SAFETY IN INDIA: Implementation is the key [Internet]. [cited 2024 Oct 4]. Available from: https://www.nimhans.ac.in/wp-content/uploads/2019/09/Advancing-Child-Safety-in-India-Implementation-is-the-Key.-A-report-by-NIMHANS-2019.pdf

2. Judy K. Unintentional Injuries in Pediatrics. Pediatrics in Review. 2011 Sep 30;32(10):431–9.

3. Serinelli S, Gitto L, Arunkumar P. Five-year review (2014-2019) of paediatric accidental deaths in Cook County, Illinois (USA). Med Leg J. 2023 Dec;91(4):186-192

4. Cunningham RM, Walton MA, Carter PM. The Major Causes of Death in Children and Adolescents in the United States. New England Journal of Medicine [Internet]. 2018 Dec 20;379(25):2468–75. Available from: https://www.nejm.org/doi/full/10.1056/nejmsr1804754

<u>SECTION II: Awareness activities</u>

1. Electricity (e.g., electrical sockets, appliances)

2. Fire safety (e.g., candles, gas stoves, firecrackers)

3. Water safety (e.g., swimming pools, bathtubs)

4. Choking hazards (e.g., marbles, small objects, food)

5. Pet safety (e.g., avoiding bites)

6. Medicine safety (e.g., taking medicine as prescribed, avoiding unfamiliar pills)

7. Poisoning hazards (e.g., cleaning chemicals, poisonous plants and animals)

8. Traffic safety (e.g., road safety rules, train safety)

9. Stranger danger (e.g., refusing gifts from strangers)

10. The dangers of smoking and alcohol

11. Baby safety tips (e.g., safe sleep, avoiding choking hazards)

"Change is not an event,
it's a process"

Hello children...

Myself superhero Scientia. I protect children from the supervillain Accido. He harms children with his evil power of causing accidents. Now you may wonder why he hurts only children and not adults. Super villain Accido cannot hurt adults because I protect adults with my "Scientia" shield. This shield gives knowledge of Accido's weapons to adults before Accido can hurt them. This also means adults who don't have Scientia shield are also vulnerable to an attack by Accido. In this book I will give you knowledge of various places where the super-villain Accido could hurt you. This will help you to recognize the attack of Accido before he can hurt you. You have to spread this knowledge to your friends and family so that they will remain protected from the attack of super villain Accido.

How to use this book…

On the next page onwards, information and sketches of various places where super villain Accido gets the opportunity to attack is given. You have to identify and memorize these places. Once you have identified all the hazards, supervillain Accido will never get the opportunity to hurt you.

<u>ACTIVITY: 1</u>

It was a hot summer day, and Raj was playing in the laundry room with the washing machine. His mother, Mrs. Jones, was in the kitchen, making dinner.

Suddenly, there was a flash of light, and Accido, the supervillain, appeared in the laundry room. He was a short, stocky man with a green face and a rounded nose. He was wearing a black cape and a hat with a skull on it.

"Hello, Raj," Accido said. "I'm here to play with you."

Raj was scared, but he didn't want to show it. "Okay," he said.

Accido picked up Raj and put him in the washing machine. "Let's see how much fun you have in here," he said.

He started the washing machine, and Raj started to scream.

Mrs. Jones heard Raj screaming and ran into the laundry room. "What's going on?" she asked.

"Accido is trying to hurt Raj," said Accido.

"Get away from my son!" Mrs. Jones shouted.

Accido laughed. "You can't stop me," he said.

Just then, there was another flash of light, and Scientia, the superhero, appeared in the laundry room. He was a handsome man with short brown hair and green eyes. He was wearing a blue costume with a red cape.

"Accido," Scientia said. "You're under arrest."

"Not today, Scientia," Accido said.

He started to fight Scientia, but he was no match for him. Scientia quickly defeated him, but Accido managed to escape.

"You'll never catch me, Scientia!" Accido shouted as he ran away.

"I'll get you next time, Accido," Scientia said.

Scientia turned to Raj and his mother. "Are you okay?" he asked.

"Yes, thank you," said Mrs. Jones. "You saved our son."

"You're welcome," said Scientia. "That's what I do."

Raj was safe, thanks to Scientia. He knew that he could always count on him to protect him from danger. And he also knew that he needed to be more careful around machinery in the future.

"Scientia," Raj said. "Thank you for saving me."

"You're welcome, Raj," Scientia said. "But next time, please be more careful around machinery. They can be dangerous if you're not careful."

"I will," Raj said. "I promise."

Scientia smiled. "That's good," he said.

Maze Puzzle 1:

<u>Puzzle 2</u>

In 1879, Sir Thomas Edison used me to light bulb. People usually extract me from the water current to make living easy, but I can hurt people if they touch me with bare hands. Who am I?
Answer: Electricity. Electricity has become an integral part of our lives. It lights bulbs, powers home appliances etc. We use wiring and electric sockets present in our home to draw this electricity for our use. But do you know electricity has the capacity to injure us if we touch it with our bare hands. This is the favourite weapon of supervillain Accido to hurt children. So, all of us should be careful whenever we use electric appliances.

<u>Puzzle 3: Color the sketch and identify the hazard!!!</u>

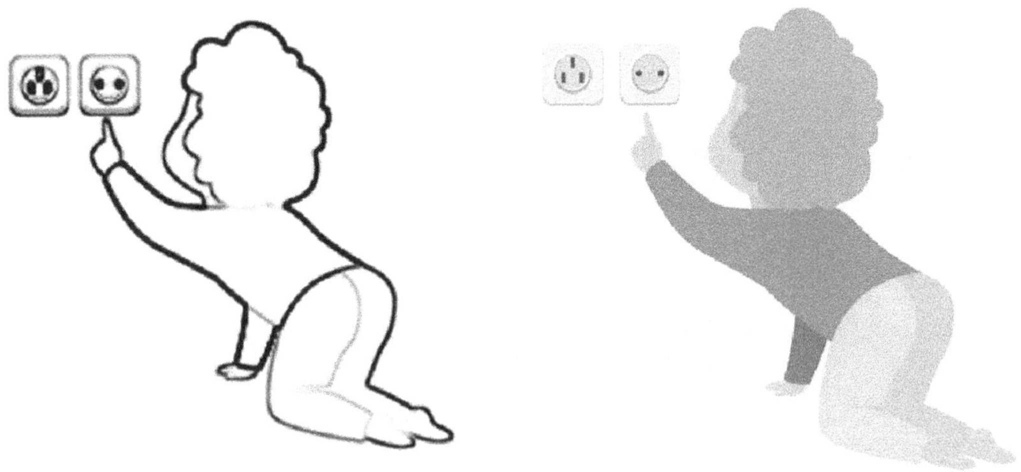

Answer: A baby is going towards an electric socket. We need to stop her as in the holes of the socket, the electric current is present and if the baby touches it, super villain Accido will get the chance to hurt her.

<u>Educate your family and friends about these safety tips:</u>

1. All electric sockets should be at least 5 ft above the level of ground.
2. Whenever possible, electric appliances should be kept on the table with a minimum height of 3 ft and appliances should be kept away from the edge of the table.
3. All tables, cabinets, almirah should be strongly fixed to the ground.

ACTIVITY: 2

Raj was still shaken up from his encounter with Accido, but he was also curious about the electric socket. He had never seen one before, and he wanted to know what it was.

He slowly reached out to touch it, but before he could, Scientia appeared.

"Raj, don't touch that!" Scientia said. "It's dangerous."

"But what is it?" Raj asked.

"It's an electric socket," Scientia said. "It's used to connect electrical appliances to the power grid."

"But why is it dangerous?" Raj asked.

"Because if you touch it, you could get electrocuted," Scientia said. "That means you could get a really bad shock that could even kill you."

Raj's eyes widened. "Really?" he asked.

"Yes," Scientia said. "So please, don't touch it."

Raj nodded. "Okay," he said. "I won't."

Raj said. "Thanks to you."

"You're welcome," Scientia said. "But I think there's something else you need to know."

"What is it?" Raj asked.

"Accido didn't just try to electrocute you," Scientia said. "He put a thought into your mind to touch the electric socket."

"What?" Raj asked. "How did he do that?"

"He's a supervillain and he can make people do things against their will."

Raj was shocked. "I didn't know that," he said.

"That's why I stopped you from touching the electric socket," Scientia said. "I knew that Accido was controlling you."

"Thank you," Raj said. "I don't know what I would have done if you hadn't been there."

"You're welcome," Scientia said. "That's what I do."

Scientia then flew away, and Raj and his mother were safe.

Raj learned his lesson about electric sockets, and he was grateful to Scientia for saving his life. He knew that he could always count on Scientia to protect him from danger.

Maze Puzzle 1:

<u>**Puzzle 2:**</u>

"I am present in every house, I need electricity to work, I make all work easy for humans, but when someone misuses me, super villain Accido gets the chance to hurt him. Guess who am I?
The answer is machines/ electric appliances. Machines have been discovered to make the work of humans easy. Almost all machines need external power supply to work. Machines draw this power from electricity. So, if we don't use these machines properly, we can get trapped in any moving part of the machine or we may get hurt due to the electric supply of the machine.

<u>**Puzzle 3: Color the sketch and identify the hazard!!!**</u>

Answer: In the above photograph a girl is playing with a toaster and her brother is trying to stop her.   The toaster works on electric current. If she keeps playing with it, she may get hurt because of electric current or any moving part of that machine.

Answer: In the above picture, a baby is going near the iron. We need to stop the baby from getting near the table. That table could fall on her. That baby may sustain burn injuries because of hot iron. Iron works on electricity, so again, that baby can get hurt because of electric current.

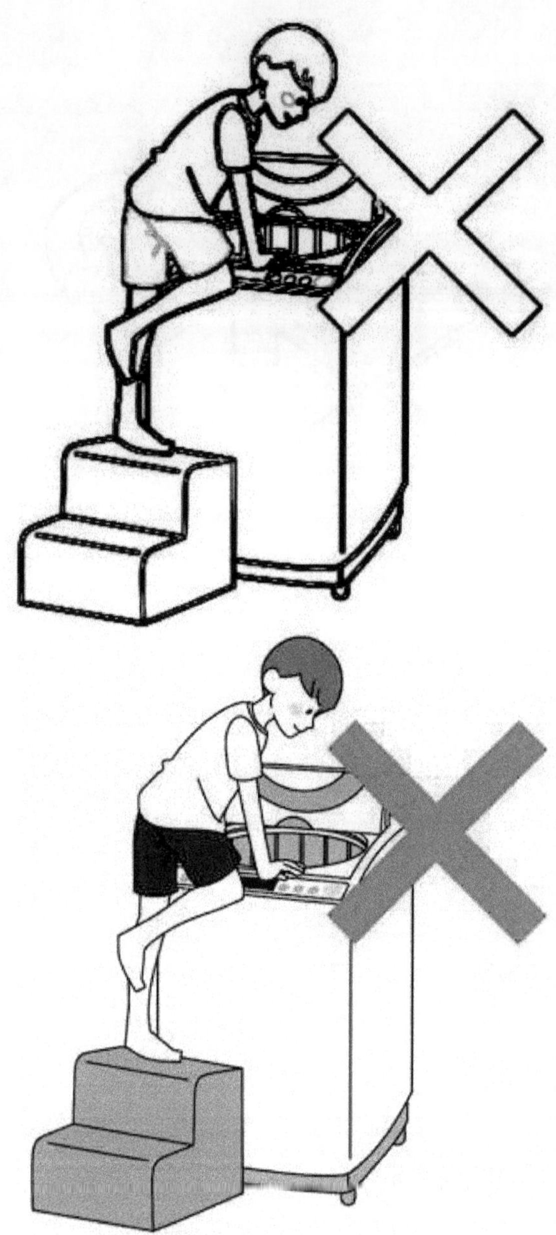

Answer: In the above picture, a boy is playing near the washing machine. We need to stop him from playing near or with the washing machine. He may get trapped inside a machine if the lid of the machine closes accidentally. The washing machine works on electricity, so again, a boy may get hurt because of electric current.

ACTIVITY: 3

The next day, Accido struck again. He caused a power outage in Raj's neighborhood, and the whole area was plunged into darkness.

Raj's mother lit a candle to provide some light, but Raj was curious about the flame. He had never seen fire before, and he wanted to know more about it.

He picked up the candle and held it close to a piece of paper. The paper started to smolder, and Raj quickly dropped the candle.

"Raj, be careful!" his mother shouted. "You could have started a fire!"

Raj was startled. "I didn't mean to," he said. "I just wanted to see what would happen."

"You need to be more careful," his mother said. "Fire is a dangerous thing."

"I know," Raj said. "I'm sorry."

Just then, Scientia appeared. He was wearing a helmet with a flashlight on it, so he could see in the darkness.

"What's going on?" Scientia asked.

"Raj was playing with the candle," his mother said. "He almost started a fire."

"I see," Scientia said. "Well, now you know why it's important to keep a safe distance between fire and inflammable materials."

"Yes," Raj said. "I understand."

"Good," Scientia said. "Now, let's get you and your mother to a safe place."

Scientia led Raj and his mother to a neighbor's house, where they could stay until the power was restored.

While they were at the neighbor's house, Scientia talked to Raj about fire safety. He explained the dangers of fire and how to prevent it.

Raj listened carefully, and he learned a lot from Scientia. He knew that he would never forget what Scientia had taught him.

The next day, the power was restored, and Raj and his mother went home. Raj was glad to be home, and he was even more glad to have learned about fire safety from Scientia.

He knew that he would always be careful around fire, and he was grateful to Scientia for helping him to learn about it.

Maze Puzzle 1:

Hazards:
Fire,
Gas stove,
Cylinder,
Fire cracker

Safe zone

Puzzle 2:

If I eat, I am fine, but if I drink water I will die. Who am I?
Answer: Fire. Fire is an integral part of our life. In winter it gives warmth, in darkness it gives light. It also helps to cook food, but if we get in direct contact with fire, it can burn and hurt us. So always maintain a safe distance from fire.

Answer: In the above photograph a candle is kept on books. Lots of papers are present in nearby candles. They could catch fire. Always keep candles or any other burning or inflammable material in a safe place and properly guarded.

Puzzle 4: Color the sketch and identify the hazard!!!

Answer: In the above picture, one child is playing with the gas stove. No one should play with the gas stove. The gas stove works on the gas flowing from the cylinder. This gas is highly inflammable. If the stove knob is kept on it will cause the spread of gas in the entire surrounding area, which may cause fire in house and injuries to people inside it.

Puzzle 5: Color the sketch and identify the hazard!!!

In the above photograph, few people are celebrating birthday with firecrackers on cake. What advice will you give them?
Answer: Firecrackers should not be used inside home. Fire crackers are made from chemicals like phosphorus. These chemicals are not only poisonous but also highly inflammable. Sudden ignition of these firecrackers can cause burning of the face, loss of eye sight and fire in house. Children less than 3 years old have a frequent habit of keeping things in their mouth, so phosphorus present in firecrackers can cause poisoning.

Educate your family and friends about these safety tips:

1. Safe place and proper precautions for inflammable materials like matches, lighters.
2. Reduce water heater temperature to 49^0C
3. Strictly avoid cooking, boiling, drinking hot liquid near children.
4. Never leave the gas stove unattended
5. Children should stay away from fireplaces, pot handles, appliance cords.
6. Increased installation of smoke detectors and monthly testing of the same
7. Improved building fire codes
8. People should be motivated to stop smoking and strictly do no smoking inside home.
9. Discuss and establish a family fire escape plan.

<u>ACTIVITY: 4</u>

Raj and his friends were playing on the ground when it started to rain. They ran to a nearby tree for shelter, but Scientia appeared and warned them about the danger of lightning strike.

"It's not safe to stand under a tree during a thunderstorm," Scientia said. "Lightning can strike trees, and if you're standing under one, you could be electrocuted."

"But where else are we supposed to go?" Raj asked. "It's raining really hard."

"You can go inside a building or a car," Scientia said. "Or you can find a low-lying area, like a ditch or a culvert."

Raj and his friends ran to find a ditch, and they waited there until the rain stopped. Scientia stayed with them, and he told them more about lightning safety.

"Lightning is a powerful electrical discharge," Scientia said. That's why it's important to be careful during thunderstorms."

"We'll be careful," Raj said.

"Good," Scientia said. "I'm glad I could help."

After the rain stopped, Raj and his friends went back to playing. They were all grateful to Scientia for teaching them about lightning safety, and they knew that they would be more careful in the future.

<u>Maze Puzzle 1:</u>

Hazards:
Lightning-
Rain- Storm

<u>Puzzle 2:</u>

I flash but I am not a camera, I roar but am not a Lion, I am white and I hide in the clouds but I am not a star. Who am I?

Answer: Lightning. During a storm, turbulence in the cloud causes the formation of positive and negative charges in the cloud. Negative charge is present at the base of the cloud while positive charge is present at the top of the cloud. When this negative charge flows towards positive charge externally, it is visible as lightning. Here one interesting thing is our earth also acts as positive charge, so negative charge present at the base of the cloud can also flow towards the positively charged earth. In common language we call it a lightning strike. Lightning is a form of electricity and, just like electricity, it loves to flow towards low resistance, so lightning is easily attracted towards wet objects like trees. If, during a storm, you stand below a tree, then there are high chances that you may get injured because of lightning falling on the tree. That's why we always stay away from trees during a lightning storm.

Can you spot the hazard in the above picture?
Answer: In the above picture, some people are standing below a tree during a storm. Lightning is easily attracted toward wet trees, so always stay away from trees during a storm and take shelter in nearby houses. You can see in the photograph lightning falling on nearby trees.

ACTIVITY: 5

Raj and his friends were playing in the park when they saw a wobbly chair. They decided to play a game of "King of the Hill" on the chair, and Raj was the first one to climb up.

He was standing on top of the chair, laughing and shouting, when Scientia appeared.

"Raj, get down from there!" Scientia said. "That chair is unstable, and you could fall and get hurt."

"I'm fine," Raj said. "I'm not going to fall."

"But what if you do?" Scientia asked. "You could break your arm or your leg, or even worse. And playing on the terrace of buildings is also unsafe. You could fall off and get seriously injured."

Raj looked down at the ground, and he realized that Scientia was right. The chair was really wobbly, and he could easily fall off. He also thought about the fact that playing on the terrace of buildings was unsafe.

"Okay," Raj said. "I'll come down."

Raj climbed down from the chair, and Scientia talked to him about the dangers of playing on unstable things and on the terrace of buildings.

"It's not worth getting hurt," Scientia said. "There are plenty of other things to play on that are safe."

"I understand," Raj said. "I'll be more careful in the future."

Raj and his friends then went on to play on some other things that were safe, and they all had a lot of fun.

<u>Maze Puzzle 1:</u>

<u>Hazards:</u>
Height, Heavy
unstable
structures

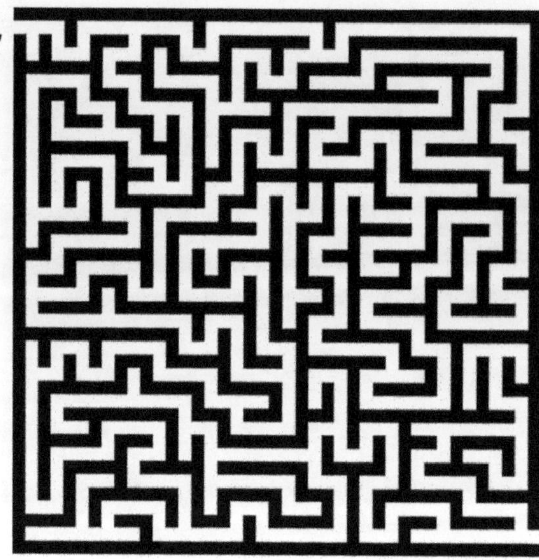

<u>Safe zone</u>

<u>Puzzle 2:</u>

One falling apple showed my existence for the first time and Sir Issac Newton was the first to notice me. I make every unstable thing fall on the earth. Who am I?

Answer: Gravity. Sir Issac Newton was the first who documented the existence of gravity after he witnessed a falling apple. Whenever we or any object lose stability, it always falls on earth instead of going in any other direction and this happens because of the gravity of the earth. Knowledge of gravity is important because when we or any objects fall there are high chances that we will sustain injury because of a fall or falling object.

Puzzle 3: Color the sketch and identify the hazard!!!

In the above picture, a person is falling from the height. Can you tell me why he is falling?

Answer: He is falling because of gravity. He was standing in the balcony and he probably lost control and fell. So, one should always be careful when he is standing in the balcony or building terrace.

Puzzle 4: Color the sketch and identify the hazard!!!

Answer: Standing and leaning over a chair or any movable object is unsafe. It can slip because of our weight, causing us to fall on the ground and sustain injury.

<u>Puzzle 5: Color the sketch and identify the hazard!!!</u>

Answer: In the above picture a girl is trying to stand over a cabinet. The cabinet is movable and not fixed, so because of the weight of that girl, it could fall over her and cause injury to her.

Puzzle 6: Color the sketch and identify the hazard!!!

Answer: In the above picture, pots are kept in the balcony. Pots or any heavy object should never be kept at the edge of the balcony as they can fall and injure the person present below it.

Educate your family and friends about these safety tips:

1. Avoid the use of baby walkers with wheels.
2. Use safety traps in high chairs, shopping carts and for diaper changes
3. Never keep heavy objects at the edge of the window, balcony or terrace.
4. Never play in the balcony or terrace.
5. Use extra precautions when you are working on height.

ACTIVITY: 6

Raj had never seen a swimming pool before, and he was excited to play in it. He had always wanted to learn how to swim, and he thought that this was the perfect opportunity.

He ran to the edge of the pool and looked down. The water was clear and blue, and it looked so inviting. Raj couldn't wait to get in.

But before he could, Scientia appeared.

"Raj, wait!" Scientia said. "You don't know how to swim. It's not safe for you to go in the pool by yourself."

"I'll be fine," Raj said. "I'll just wade in the shallow end."

"Even the shallow end can be dangerous," Scientia said. "You could slip and fall, or you could get water in your lungs and drown."

Raj looked at the pool again, and he realized that Scientia was right. He didn't know how to swim, and he could easily get hurt.

"Okay," Raj said. "I'll wait until I learn how to swim before I go in the pool."

"That's a good decision," Scientia said. "In the meantime, you can play in the sprinklers."

Raj agreed, and he went to play in the sprinklers. He had a lot of fun, and he was glad that he had listened to Scientia.

Later, Raj took swimming lessons, and he learned how to swim safely. He was so happy that he had waited to go in the pool until he knew how to swim.

Maze Puzzle 1:

Puzzle 2:

If I go into your stomach, I quench your thirst. If I go into your nose, I will not allow you to breath. I will drench you during the rain. Who am I?
Answer: Water. Whenever we are thirsty, we need water to drink. If water goes into our respiratory tract, it can hurt us. So always drink water slowly and not in a hurry to avoid it going in our respiratory tract.

Answer: In the above picture, a baby is present near a swimming pool. No adult is present near her. She can fall in swimming pool and get injured because of drowning. Children don't know how to swim and if they fall in the swimming pool they can get hurt. So always use protective measures and follow all swimming pool protocol.

Answer: In the above picture, a baby is sitting in the bathtub. Bathtub for babies should be used only in the presence of adults. Babies are not strong enough to get out of a tub and if they lose body stability in the bathtub, they can get injured. In fact, installation or use of bathtubs should be discouraged in all houses as injuries due to fall/ slip/ unconsciousness/ seizers are very common in bathtubs.

Educate your family and friends about these safety tips:

1. At least 4 ft high fencing around the pool and self-closing gate
2. Use of life jackets
3. Mandatory swimming lessons
4. Lifeguards: Adults should be present at least 1 arm's reach of a child in or near water

<u>ACTIVITY: 7</u>

Raj was playing in the hall when he saw a box of marbles. He had never seen marbles before, and he was curious about them.

He opened the box and took out a marble. The marble was smooth and round, and it felt good in his hand. He put the marble near his mouth and looked at it closely.

Just then, Scientia appeared.

"Raj, don't put that in your mouth!" Scientia said. "It's a choking hazard."

"What's a choking hazard?" Raj asked.

"It's something that can block your airway and make you choke," Scientia said. "Marbles are a choking hazard because they're small and round. If you swallow a marble, it could get stuck in your throat and block your airway."

Raj looked at the marble again, and he realized that Scientia was right. The marble was small enough to fit in his mouth, and it could easily get stuck in his throat.

"Okay," Raj said. "I'll put it down."

Raj put the marble back in the box, and Scientia talked to him about choking hazards.

"There are a lot of things that can be choking hazards," Scientia said. "It's important to be careful when you're playing with small objects, and you should never put anything in your mouth that you're not sure is safe."

"I understand," Raj said. "I'll be more careful in the future."

Raj put the box of marbles away, and he went on to play with some other toys. He was glad that he had listened to Scientia, and he knew that he would be more careful in the future.

Maze Puzzle 1:

Puzzle 2:

I am a ball. Everyone kicks me, but not because they hate me. It's a game where people try to send me to the opposition post to win. Guess my name?

Answer: Football.

Answer: In the above picture a **baby is playing** with a beaded necklace. Beads of the necklace may get lodged in the respiratory tract and cause choking. Children between 1-5 years have weak gag reflexes. So, they pose a danger of choking with small objects. So, whenever you see anyone keeping small objects like toys, marbles in their mouth or playing with them, stop them from doing so.

Puzzle 4:

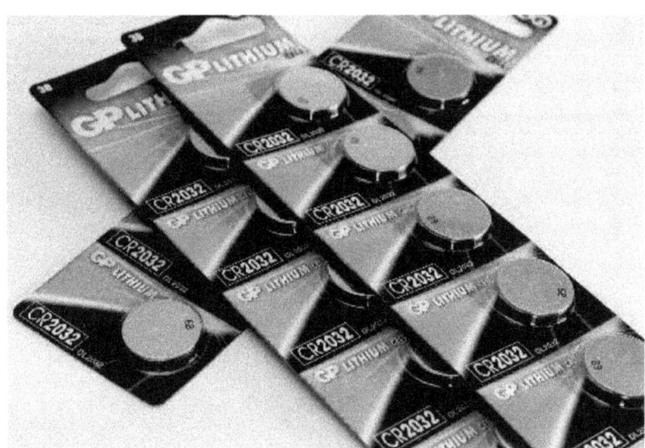

Can you solve this riddle…?
I am the movable source of power. I use chemicals to generate power. I have a head and tail. My head always thinks positively and my tail always thinks negatively. Italian physicist Sir Alessandro Volta made me operable for the first time. Guess who I am?

Answer: Battery. The battery is manufactured in different sizes and shapes and it is denoted by letters like AA, AAA, CR2032, LR 44 etc. In the common language, CR and LR batteries are also called button or coin batteries. The alphabet in battery name indicates their content, shape and potential. For example, C in CR denotes chromium lithium compound content and R denotes round. As CR and LR batteries are small and round, they pose a danger of choking or swallowing hazards to children. Just like choking, swallowing of a battery is also a medical emergency as discharge of electricity or chemicals from these batteries poses the danger of injury to the food track (gastrointestinal tract) and poisoning.

ACTIVITY: 8

Raj was eating his dinner when his friends came to the door. They were calling him to go to the playground, and Raj was excited to play with them.

He quickly finished his dinner, but he was eating so quickly that he didn't chew his food properly.

Just then, Scientia appeared.

"Raj, slow down," Scientia said. "You're not supposed to eat your food so quickly."

"But I'm in a hurry," Raj said. "I want to go play with my friends."

"I know you're in a hurry," Scientia said. "But it's important to chew your food properly. If you don't, you could choke."

"Choke?" Raj asked.

"Yes," Scientia said. "If you don't chew your food properly, it could get stuck in your throat and block your airway. That could make you choke."

Raj looked at his food, and he realized that Scientia was right. He hadn't chewed his food very well, and it could easily get stuck in his throat.

"Okay," Raj said. "I'll slow down and chew my food properly."

Raj took a few deep breaths and slowed down his eating. He chewed his food slowly and carefully, and he made sure that he swallowed it properly.

"That's better," Scientia said. "Now you can go play with your friends."

Raj went outside to play with his friends, and he had a lot of fun. He was glad that he had listened to Scientia, and he knew that he would be more careful in the future.

Here are some additional tips for eating safely:

- Sit down when you eat.
- Chew your food thoroughly.
- Don't talk while you're eating.
- Don't eat while you're walking or running.
- Avoid eating large bites.

- If you're choking, don't panic. Cough forcefully to try to dislodge the food. If you can't dislodge the food, call 112 or your local emergency number.

Maze Puzzle 1:

Puzzle 2:

I am round, but when you cut to eat me, my shape changes to sector. When you order me from a shop, I usually get delivered in 30 minutes. I don't reside in a hut, but one food shop sells me by adding a hut after my name. Guess me?

Answer: Pizza. We all love food and when it's our favourite food we can't wait to eat it. But children always keep in mind that we should eat food slowly. If we eat food in a hurried way or if we stuff our mouth with food, it can block our breathing and hurt us.

Answer: In the above photograph, a child is eating food. This child has stuffed her mouth with food and this can cause blocking of her airway. She should remove stuffed food from her mouth and eat it slowly.

ACTIVITY: 9

Raj was playing in the kitchen when he saw the stove. He had never seen a stove before, and he was curious about it.

He turned on the stove and watched the flames flicker. He thought it was cool, so he started turning the stove on and off.

Just then, Scientia appeared.

"Raj, don't play with the stove!" Scientia said. "It's dangerous."

"But it's so cool!" Raj said. "I like watching the flames."

"I know it's cool," Scientia said. "But it's also dangerous. If you leave the stove on, it could cause a fire."

"A fire?" Raj asked.

"Yes," Scientia said. "A fire is a very dangerous thing. It can burn your house down, and it can even hurt you."

Raj looked at the stove, and he realized that Scientia was right. He could easily start a fire if he wasn't careful.

"Okay," Raj said. "I'll stop playing with the stove."

Raj turned off the stove and went to sit down. Scientia talked to him about the dangers of playing with stoves.

"Stoves are very powerful appliances," Scientia said. "They can cause a lot of damage if they're not used properly. That's why it's important to never play with stoves, and to always be careful when you're using them."

"I understand," Raj said. "I'll be more careful in the future."

Raj learned a valuable lesson that day. He learned that it's important to be careful around stoves, and that playing with them can be dangerous. He was grateful to Scientia for teaching him this lesson, and he knew that he would be more careful in the future.

<u>**Maze Puzzle 1:**</u>

Hazards:
Gas stove,
Cylinder

<u>**Safe zone**</u>

<u>**Puzzle 2:**</u>

I am a place in the house where mommy and daddy cook nutritious food for all family. When you are hungry you always go into this room. Guess the name of this room…

Answer: Kitchen. The kitchen is the place where we keep utensils, store, wash and cook food. Apart from food and utensils, many other things like electric appliances, sharp or heavy instruments, cleaning chemicals, gas stoves are also present in kitchens. All parents should keep these things safely, at least at the minimum height of 3 feet and away from the edge of the counter or inside the cabinet (whichever is applicable).

<u>Puzzle 3: Color the sketch and identify the hazard!!!</u>

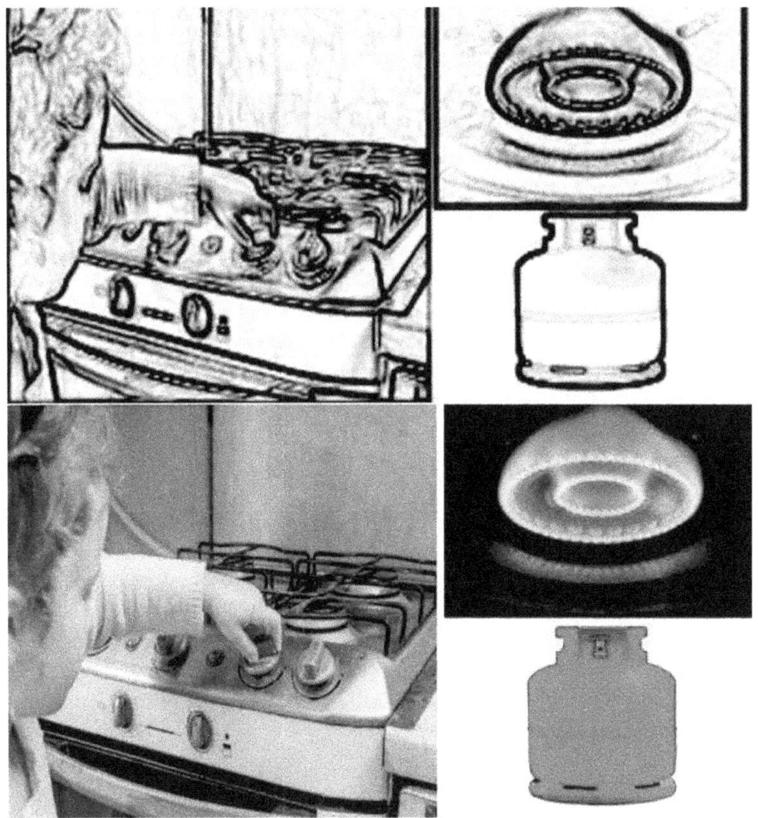

In the above picture, you can see a gas stove is easily accessible to a child. It should be kept at a sufficient height and away from the edge of the cooking counter. Similarly, gas sources should be kept sufficiently guarded from children.

ACTIVITY: 10

Raj was playing with his pet dog, Dumdum, in the backyard. They were playing fetch, and Raj was having a lot of fun.

After a while, Raj got tired, so he sat down on the grass. Dumdum came over to him and licked his face. Raj laughed and petted Dumdum.

Then, Raj put his hand in Dumdum's mouth. Dumdum started to chew on Raj's hand, and Raj laughed again.

Just then, Scientia appeared.

"Raj, don't put your hands in Dumdum's mouth!" Scientia said. "It's not safe."

"But he's just playing," Raj said.

"I know he's just playing," Scientia said. "But dogs can have sharp teeth, and they can accidentally bite you. Even if Dumdum doesn't mean to hurt you, he could still do some damage."

Raj looked at his hand, and he realized that Scientia was right. Dumdum's teeth were sharp, and he could easily bite Raj if he wasn't careful.

"Okay," Raj said. "I'll stop putting my hands in Dumdum's mouth."

Raj pulled his hand out of Dumdum's mouth and went to sit down. Scientia talked to him about being careful around animals.

"It's important to be careful around all animals," Scientia said. "Even if they're your pets, they can still hurt you if they're not properly trained. That's why it's important to never put your hands in an animal's mouth, and to always be aware of your surroundings when you're around animals."

"I understand," Raj said. "I'll be more careful in the future."

Raj learned a valuable lesson that day. He learned that it's important to be careful around animals, and that putting his hands in an animal's mouth can be dangerous. He was grateful to Scientia for teaching him this lesson, and he knew that he would be more careful in the future.

Here are some additional tips for staying safe around animals:

- **Never approach an animal that you don't know.**
- **Always ask the owner's permission before petting an animal.**
- **Be aware of your surroundings when you're around animals.**
- **Don't put your hands in an animal's mouth.**
- **If an animal bites you, seek medical attention immediately.**

Maze Puzzle 1:

Puzzle 2:

They are lovely, they are innocent, they are just like babies. They have four legs and a tail. They love us and show their love by waggling their tail. Who are they?

Answer: Pets. We all love pets. Pets love us unconditionally but they do not have capacity to think properly. Always be careful while spending time with them and never tease them. Pets are harmless if we love them and at the same time if we keep safe distance from them. (Here the word safe distance means do not tease them, take good medical care etc)

Answer: In the above picture a boy is playing with his pet. Boy is putting hand in the mouth of his pet. This should not be done. His hand may get injured by accidental teeth bite of his pet. This may be dangerous for boy if pet is having any infection.

ACTIVITY: 11

Raj was watching a Superman movie with his friends. He was so excited to see Superman flying, and he wished he could fly like him.

After the movie, Raj's friends went home, but Raj stayed up late thinking about Superman. He wanted to be a superhero like Superman, and he wanted to be able to fly.

The next day, Raj was playing in the backyard when Scientia appeared.

"Raj," Scientia said. "I know you're excited about Superman, but you need to know that he's not real."

"What do you mean?" Raj asked. "I saw him in the movie."

"The movies are fictional," Scientia said. "They're produced with the help of computer technology. It's not possible for humans to fly."

Raj was disappointed. He had really wanted to be able to fly like Superman.

"But I want to be a superhero," Raj said.

"You can be a superhero," Scientia said. "But you don't need to fly to be a superhero. A real superhero is someone who does good work and helps others. It's about being kind and compassionate, and it's about making a difference in the world."

Raj thought about what Scientia said. He knew that she was right. He didn't need to fly to be a superhero. He could be a superhero by doing good work and helping others.

"I'll be a superhero," Raj said. "I'll do good work and help others."

Raj went on to become a great superhero. He helped people in need, and he made the world a better place. He didn't fly, but he was still a superhero.

Maze Puzzle 1:

Hazards:
False belief-
Rumours

Safe zone

<u>Puzzle 2:</u>

What is the word used for a condition where a person has false belief in something whose falsity has already been proved?
Answer: Delusion. Many times, we watch something on television or the media and start believing in it. Do not believe in unrealistic things without proper proof. For example, we watch super heroes flying in movies, but in real life it's not possible for any human to fly without the help of a machine. In movies, special computerized software is used to show humans flying. You can see the photograph below; a man is lying prone on a chair and in the next photograph, with the help of a computer chair is erased from the photograph so that man looks like he is flying.

ACTIVITY: 12

Raj and his friends were playing in the hall when Raj spotted a plastic bag. He had never seen a plastic bag before, and he was curious about it.

He picked up the plastic bag and put it over his head. He thought it was cool, and he started to breathe through the bag.

Just then, Scientia appeared.

"Raj, take that bag off your head!" Scientia said. "It's dangerous!"

"But it's so cool!" Raj said. "I like breathing through it."

"I know it's cool," Scientia said. "But it's also dangerous. If you breathe in the plastic, it could block your airways and suffocate you."

"Suffocate?" Raj asked.

"Yes," Scientia said. "Suffocation is when you can't breathe. It's a very dangerous thing, and it can kill you."

Raj looked at the plastic bag, and he realized that Scientia was right. He could easily suffocate if he wasn't careful.

"Okay," Raj said. "I'll take it off."

Raj took the plastic bag off his head and went to sit down. Scientia talked to him about the dangers of putting plastic bags over your head.

"Plastic bags are very dangerous," Scientia said. "They can block your airways and suffocate you. That's why it's important to never put a plastic bag over your head, and to always dispose of plastic bags properly."

"I understand," Raj said. "I'll be more careful in the future."

Raj learned a valuable lesson that day. He learned that it's important to be careful around plastic bags, and that putting plastic bags over your head can be dangerous. He was grateful to Scientia for teaching him this lesson, and he knew that he would be more careful in the future.

Here are some additional tips for staying safe around plastic bags:

- **Never put a plastic bag over your head.**

- **Never leave a plastic bag where a child or pet can reach it.**
- **Dispose of plastic bags properly by recycling them or putting them in the trash.**
- **If you see a child or pet playing with a plastic bag, take it away from them immediately.**

Maze Puzzle 1:

Hazards:
Plastic bags,
Window blind
cord

Safe zone

Puzzle 2:

I am everywhere. I contain gases like oxygen and carbon dioxide. All living things use me to breath. Who am I?

Answer: Air. All living things need oxygen to survive and they take oxygen by breathing air through their nose. If our nose and mouth is blocked, then it's not possible to breathe.

<u>Puzzle 3:</u>

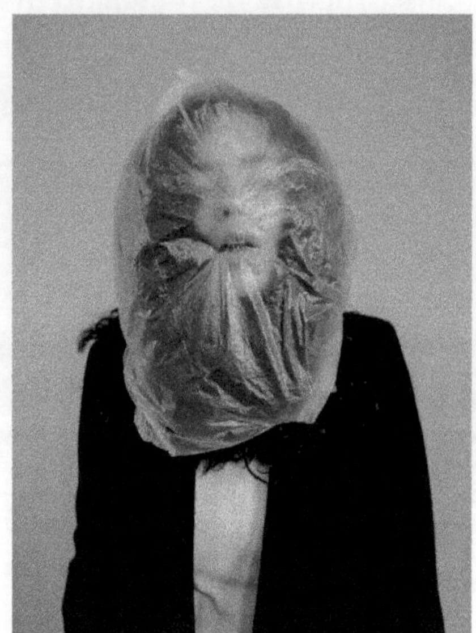

Can you spot the hazard in the above picture?
Answer: In the above picture, the head of a girl is covered in plastic. Plastic can block her nose and mouth and injure her. Because of electrostatic forces, plastic has the ability to get easily attached to our skin. So, it can block the nose and mouth, causing suffocation. Always remember. Never put your head in plastic or any closed bag.

<u>Puzzle 4: Color the sketch and identify the hazard!!!</u>

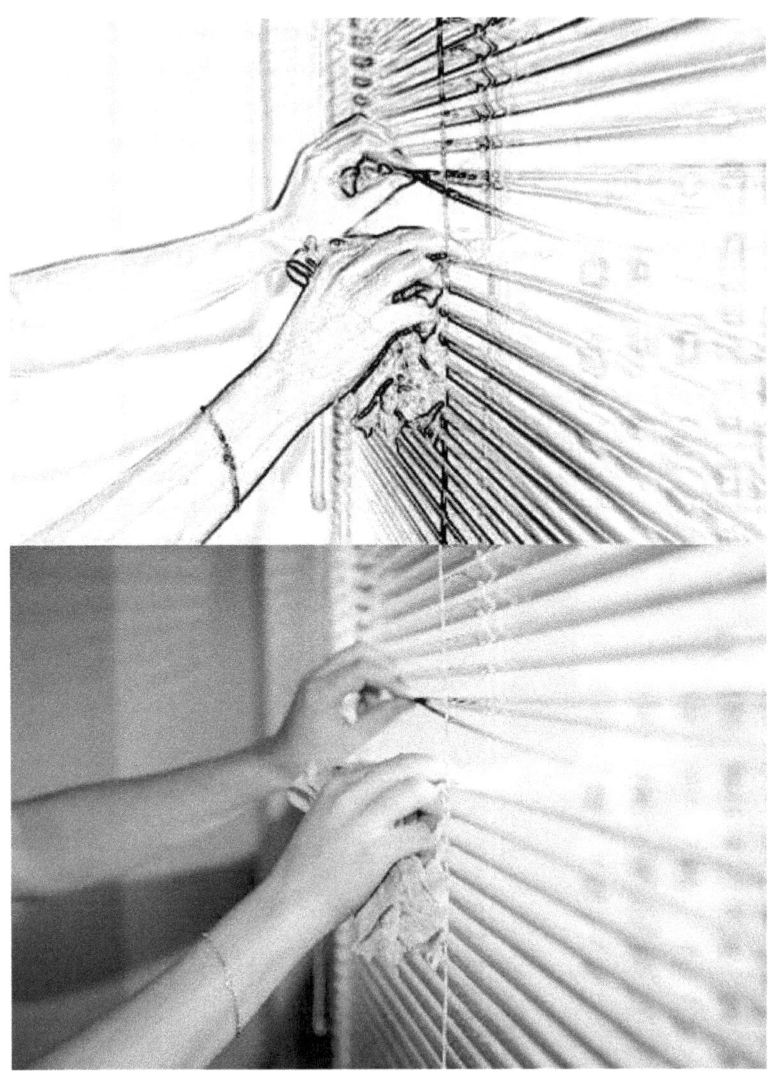

Do you know the name of this curtain used over the window in the above picture?

Answer: It is called as window blind cord. This type of curtain is highly dangerous for children and it should never be used in houses. They are dangerous because the neck of a child may get trapped between the layers of blind cord and may cause serious injury to children.

ACTIVITY: 13

Raj was feeling sick, so his mother took him to the doctor. The doctor examined Raj and diagnosed him with a cold. He prescribed Raj some pills to help him get better.

Raj's mother gave him the pills, but Raj refused to take them. He said that they were bitter and he didn't want to take them.

"You need to take the pills," his mother said. "They'll help you get better."

"But they're bitter!" Raj said. "I don't want to take them."

"I know they're bitter," his mother said. "But they're the only way to make you better."

Raj still refused to take the pills. He was determined not to take them, no matter what.

Just then, Scientia appeared.

"Raj," Scientia said. "I know you don't want to take the pills, but you need to."

"Why?" Raj asked.

"Because they'll help you get better," Scientia said. "The doctor prescribed them for a reason. They're the best way to cure your cold."

Raj thought about what Scientia said. He knew that she was right. He needed to take the pills if he wanted to get better.

"Okay," Raj said. "I'll take the pills."

Raj took the pills, and he started to feel better soon after. He was grateful to Scientia for helping him understand the importance of taking medicine, and he knew that he would be more compliant in the future.

<u>Maze Puzzle 1:</u>

<u>Hazards:</u>
Infection-
Quacks

<u>Safe zone</u>

<u>Puzzle 2:</u>

We cause all the types of infections. We usually reside in unhygienic person and whenever other humans fail to take proper precautions; we get opportunity to infect them. Who are we?

Answer: Pathogen also called as harmful microorganisms. Illiterate people think infections are caused by magic but actually they are caused by very small microorganisms. With the advancement of science now medicines are available for almost all types of infections caused by microorganisms and only need is we should start treatment of the infection as early as possible.

Puzzle 3: Color the sketch and identify the hazard!!

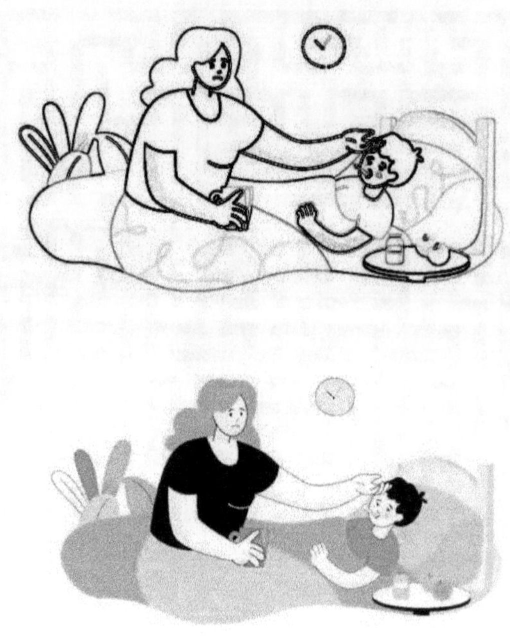

Puzzle 4: Color the sketch and identify the hazard!!!

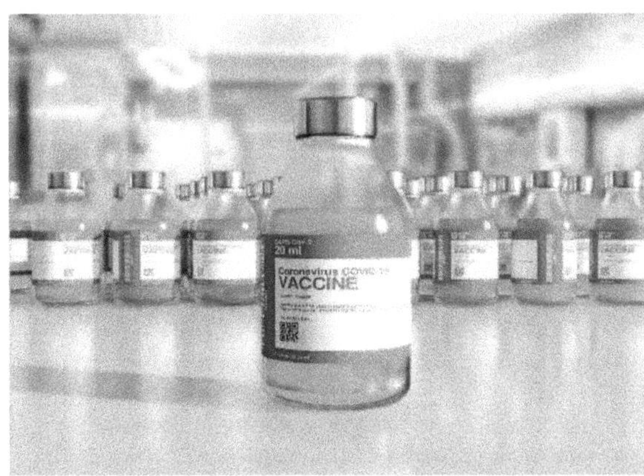

Educate your family and friends about these safety tips:

1. Infections are caused by microorganism.
2. Infections can be easily cured if we start treatment as early as possible
3. Always take treatment from qualified doctors.
4. Real magic does not exist, so never go to magician for treatment of disease.
5. Now a days there are medicines available called vaccines which gives us protection even if we are exposed to harmful microorganism.
6. Vaccines are totally safe and they don't have any harmful side effects. (Authors of this book has taken all recommended vaccines and they are completely fit and healthy.)

ACTIVITY: 14

Maze Puzzle 1:

Paracelsus has said "Sola dosis facit venenum." In simple words, it means anything in excess can cause harmful effects on our body. Paracelsus, who is also called the father of toxicology, has observed that substances which are beneficial for our health in small quantities can become harmful if those substances are consumed in more than recommended quantities. The same principle applies to medicine. Medicine helps us to cure diseases, but if we do not follow instructions for those medicines, they can harm us. Whenever you take medicine, always check for the following things on the label of the medicine. Follow these instructions.

Educate your family and friends about these safety tips:

1. Recommended dose (always take dose as per doctor's prescription)
2. Timing of medication and route of administration (always take as per doctor's prescription)
3. Whether medicine has any side effects or drug interaction (usually the doctor tells you this at the time of prescribing medicine)
4. Always check the expiry date and storage information of medicine on the label.
5. Always keep medicine in a safe place, away from the reach of children.
6. All medicines should have labels.
7. Expired medicine, medicines without labels should be discarded safely.
8. Never take medicine without a doctor's advice (avoid self-medication). Some viral illnesses are self-limiting and they require simple care and precautions. If medicines are used without a doctor's advice, it may result in unnecessary medication and its side effects: antibiotic resistance, toxicity, wrong medication, wrong doses, delayed treatment of serious illness etc
9. Always keep the poison control centre number handy.

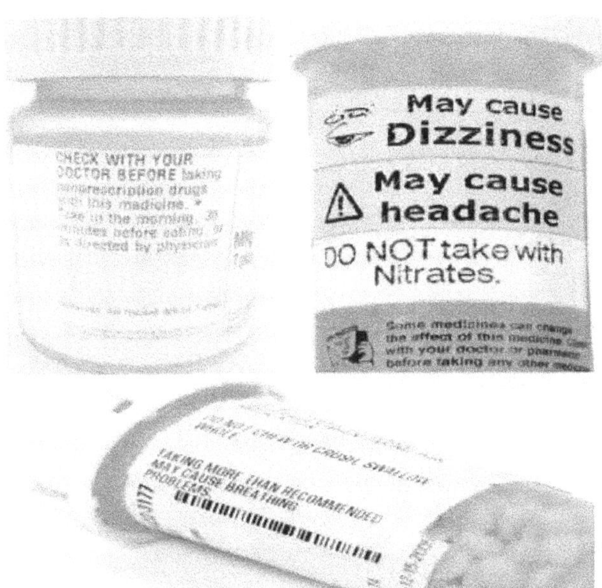

CHECK WITH YOUR DOCTOR BEFORE taking
nonprescription drugs with this medicine.
May cause
Dizziness
May cause
headache
DO NOT take with Nitrates.
TAKING MORE THAN RECOMMENDED
MAY CAUSE BREATHING PROBLEMS.

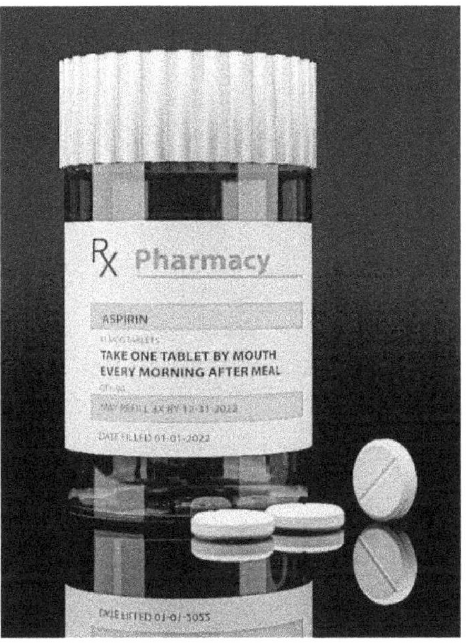

Rx Pharmacy
ASPIRIN
TAKE ONE TABLET BY MOUTH
EVERY MORNING AFTER MEAL

ACTIVITY: 15

Raj was playing in the house when he spotted his mother's medications. He had never seen them before, and he was curious about them.

He picked up the bottle of pills and looked at them. They were small and round, and they had a strange smell.

Raj was about to put one of the pills in his mouth when Scientia appeared.

"Raj, don't touch those pills!" Scientia said. "They're not for you."

"Why not?" Raj asked.

"Because they're medicine," Scientia said. "They're not for kids to play with."

"But they look so interesting," Raj said.

"I know they look interesting," Scientia said. "But they're also dangerous. If you take them, you could get sick."

Raj looked at the pills again, and he realized that Scientia was right. They were dangerous. He didn't want to get sick, so he put them back in the bottle.

"Okay," Raj said. "I won't touch them."

Scientia smiled. "Good," she said. "Now, I want to talk to your mother about keeping her medications in a safe place."

Scientia turned to Raj's mother, who was standing in the doorway.

"Mrs. Smith," Scientia said. "It's important to keep your medications in a safe place where Raj can't get to them. If he takes them, he could get sick."

Raj's mother nodded. "I understand," she said. "I'll put them away right now."

Raj's mother took the bottle of pills and put it in a high cabinet where Raj couldn't reach it.

"Thank you," Scientia said. "It's important to keep children safe."

Scientia then turned to Raj.

"Raj," Scientia said. "I'm glad you listened to me. It's important to be careful around medications. They're not toys."

Raj nodded. "I know," he said. "I won't touch them again."

Raj and his mother were both grateful to Scientia for helping them to stay safe. They knew that they would be more careful in the future.

Maze Puzzle 1:

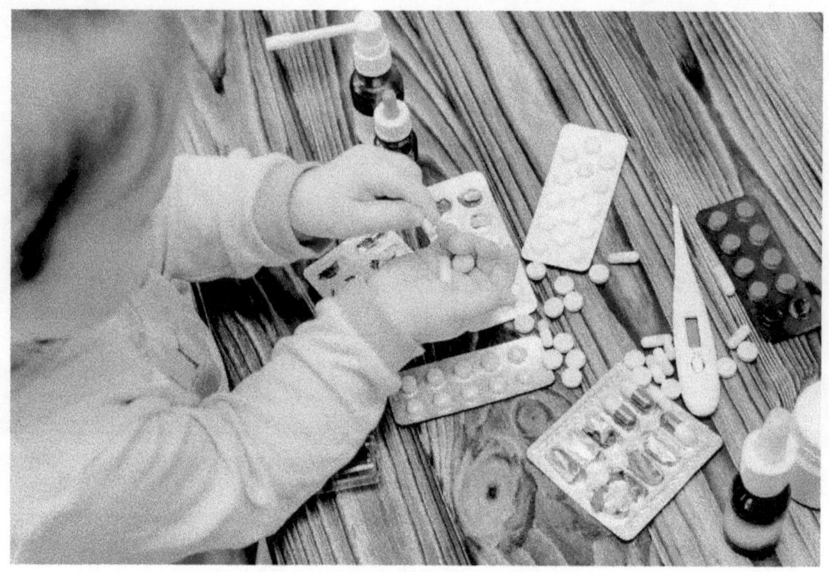

Puzzle 2: Spot the hazard in above picture
Answer: In this picture you can see medicine are easily accessible to a child. This may pose danger to his life if he swallows those medicine. Always keep medicine in safe and guarded place.

Puzzle 3: Color the sketch and identify the hazard!!!

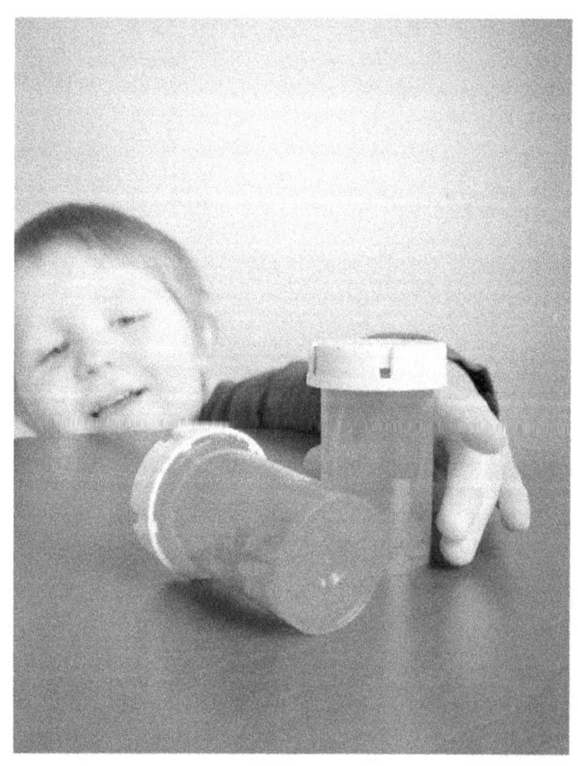

ACTIVITY: 16

Raj was playing in the house when he spotted his mother's cleaning chemicals. He had never seen them before, and he was curious about them.

He picked up the bottle of cleaning solution and looked at it. It was clear and smelled strong.

Raj was about to put some of the cleaning solution on his hands when Scientia appeared.

"Raj, don't touch that!" Scientia said. "It's not for you."

"Why not?" Raj asked.

"Because it's cleaning chemicals," Scientia said. "They're not for kids to play with."

"But they look so interesting," Raj said.

"I know they look interesting," Scientia said. "But they're also dangerous. If you get them on your skin, they can burn you. And if you swallow them, they can make you sick."

Raj looked at the cleaning solution again, and he realized that Scientia was right. They were dangerous. He didn't want to get hurt, so he put the bottle back down.

"Okay," Raj said. "I won't touch it."

Scientia smiled. "Good," she said. "Now, I want to talk to your mother about keeping her cleaning chemicals in a safe place."

Scientia turned to Raj's mother, who was standing in the doorway.

"Mrs. Smith," Scientia said. "It's important to keep your cleaning chemicals in a safe place where Raj can't get to them. If he gets them on his skin or swallows them, he could be hurt."

Raj's mother nodded. "I understand," she said. "I'll put them away right now."

Raj's mother took the bottle of cleaning solution and put it in a high cabinet where Raj couldn't reach it.

"Thank you," Scientia said. "It's important to keep children safe."

Scientia then turned to Raj.

"Raj," Scientia said. "I'm glad you listened to me. It's important to be careful around cleaning chemicals. They're not toys."

Raj nodded. "I know," he said. "I won't touch them again."

Raj and his mother were both grateful to Scientia for helping them to stay safe. They knew that they would be more careful in the future.

The end.

Here are some additional tips for keeping cleaning chemicals safe:

- **Store cleaning chemicals in a locked cabinet or cupboard.**
- **Keep cleaning chemicals out of reach of children and pets.**
- **Never leave cleaning chemicals on countertops or tables.**
- **Dispose of cleaning chemicals properly.**
- **Read and follow all safety instructions on cleaning chemical labels.**

Maze Puzzle 1:

<u>Puzzle 2:</u>

I am present in every house and humans use me to clean and disinfect houses so that everyone in the house will remain protected, but if I come in direct contact with a human body, I can hurt humans too. Who am I?
Answer: Surface disinfectant and cleaners like phenols, acids, alkalis etc.
Household chemicals are the chemicals found in products that we use in and around the house in our daily life. These include disinfectants, bleach, drain cleaners, nail polish and nail polish removers, detergents, hair dye, insect sprays and baits, lamp oils, medicines. During the early years of life, children have the habit of unknowingly putting things in their mouths and if household chemicals are kept carelessly on the ground, this poses a danger of accidental injury to children. Always keep household chemicals safely locked in a cabinet, preferably 5 feet above the level of ground.

<u>Puzzle 3: Color the sketch and identify the hazard!!!</u>

Answer: One child is sitting on the ground and behind him household chemicals are kept in the open which are easily accessible to him. If he touches these chemicals there are chances that he may get injured.

Educate your family and friends about these safety tips:

The above picture shows signs which are usually placed in a place where harmful things are present in the surrounding area. These signs are kept there to make us aware of those dangers. Each sign gives specific information and every person should be aware of these signs.

ACTIVITY: 17

Raj and his friends were playing on the ground when Raj spotted a zigzag moving animal. He had never seen an animal like it before, and he was curious about it.

"Hey guys, look at this!" Raj said. "What is that?"

Raj's friends looked at the animal, and they were just as curious as he was.

"I don't know," one of Raj's friends said. "But it looks cool."

Raj was about to reach out and touch the animal when Scientia appeared.

"Raj, don't touch that!" Scientia said. "It's not for you."

"Why not?" Raj asked.

"Because it's an unknown animal," Scientia said. "You don't know what it is, and it could be dangerous."

"But it looks so harmless," Raj said.

"I know it looks harmless," Scientia said. "But you don't know for sure. It could have sharp teeth or claws, or it could be poisonous. It's not worth the risk."

Raj looked at the animal again, and he realized that Scientia was right. He didn't know anything about the animal, and it could be dangerous. He didn't want to get hurt, so he backed away.

"Okay," Raj said. "I won't touch it."

Scientia smiled. "Good," she said. "Now, I want to talk to you and your friends about touching unknown animals."

Scientia turned to Raj and his friends.

"It's important to be careful around unknown animals," Scientia said. "You don't know what they are, and they could be dangerous. If you see an unknown animal, it's best to leave it alone."

Raj and his friends nodded. They knew that Scientia was right.

"Thank you, Scientia," Raj said. "We'll be more careful in the future."

Raj and his friends learned a valuable lesson that day. They learned that it's important to be careful around unknown animals, and that it's best to leave them alone. They were grateful to Scientia for helping them to stay safe, and they knew that they would be more careful in the future.

Maze Puzzle 1:

Puzzle 2:

My mouth has forked tongue. With my forked tongue, I make the sound of hiss. I usually hiss before I bite. My bite may contain venom. Who am I?
Answer: Snake. Some animals naturally have poison inside their bodies and whenever you spot them, go away from them and inform your adults. Examples of poisonous animals include snakes, scorpions etc.

Just like animals, plants can also be poisonous. There are some plants which contain poison in the bodies. Having knowledge of these plants is very important.

Mushroom: Some species of mushroom are nonpoisonous and are used as food. Amanita phalloides and Amanita Muscaria are the common varieties of poisonous fungi. Poisonous mushrooms usually have a bitter, astringent, acid or salt taste, and on cut section and exposure to air change color to a brown, green or blue.

Nerium odorum also called as common oleander or Kaner: This is a garden plant with elongated leaves and has white, pink or yellow flower. All parts of this plant are poisonous. (Photo credits: Wikimedia)

Castor plant: This is a tall plant with lobate shaped leaves. Fruits are globular with soft spines on the surface. Seeds are oval and shiny and has irregular spots on surface. All parts of this plant are poisonous. (Photo credits: Wikimedia)

Calotropis: This plant has green oblong leaves and white purple flowers. Stem when break exudes milky fluid which is highly irritant. All parts of this plant are poisonous. (Photo credits: Wikimedia)

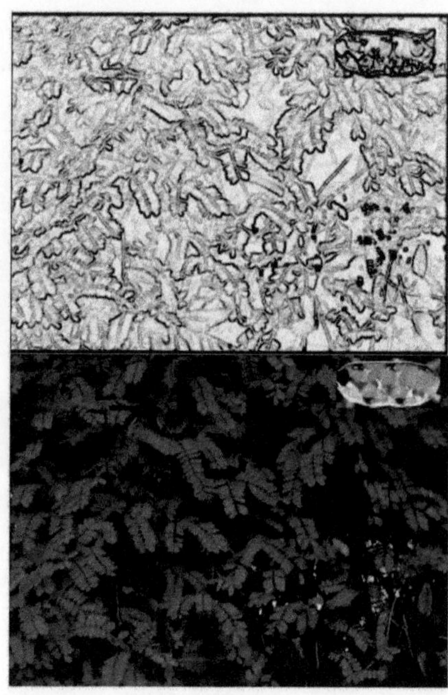

Abrus precatorius: This plant has green compound leaves and oval seeds are present in seed pot. Color of seed depends on species. Seeds may be red or white with black spot at end or black with white spot at end. All parts of this plant are poisonous. (Photo credits: Wikimedia)

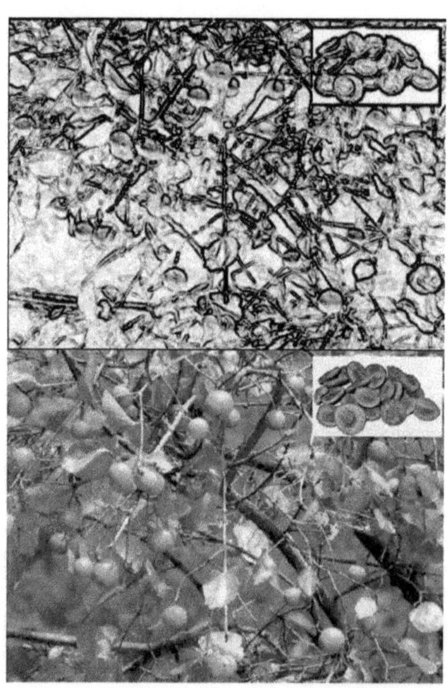

Strychnous nux vomica plant: This plant has oval dark green leaves and globular fruits with disc shaped seeds. All parts of this plant are poisonous. (Photo credits: Wikimedia)

ACTIVITY: 18

Raj and his friends were playing on the road. They were playing tag, and they were having a lot of fun.

Suddenly, Scientia appeared.

"Raj, don't play on the road!" Scientia said. "It's not safe."

"Why not?" Raj asked. "We're having fun."

"Because the road is meant for transportation," Scientia said. "There are cars and trucks that go very fast, and they could hit you if you're not careful."

"But we're careful," Raj said. "We're always watching out for cars."

"You may be careful, but other people might not be," Scientia said. "And it only takes one mistake to get hurt. It's not worth the risk."

Raj looked at the road, and he realized that Scientia was right. It wasn't safe to play on the road. He didn't want to get hurt, so he stopped playing.

"Okay," Raj said. "We'll play somewhere else."

Raj and his friends moved to a park, where they could play safely. They were grateful to Scientia for helping them to stay safe, and they knew that they would be more careful in the future.

Here are some additional tips for staying safe on the road:

- **Always look both ways before crossing the street.**
- **Never play in the street.**
- **Be aware of your surroundings when you're walking or biking.**
- **Obey traffic laws.**
- **Don't drink and drive.**

Maze Puzzle 1:

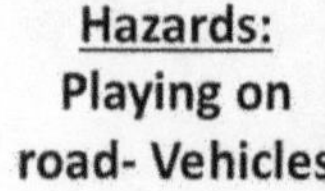

Puzzle 2:

I make transport easy. I save time for people who use me. If I have a pothole on me, then driving becomes difficult. I am safe when you follow the rules, but you may get hurt if you don't follow the rules. Who am I?

Answer: Road.

<u># Puzzle 3: Color the sketch and identify the hazard!!!</u>

Everyone likes good roads for traveling. Good roads save us time as well as they protect our vehicles from damage. When the road is unclean, it has potholes and no safety measures, they can cause damage to our vehicle and discomfort to us. Clean and safe roads can also cause injury to us if we don't follow road safety rules and don't keep awareness while using it. As shown in the above picture, always use a footpath when you are walking on the road. If traffic lights are present, then use the road as per traffic signal. Always use zebra lines (if present) to cross roads. Before crossing roads, make sure it is safe to cross by looking right and left. Never walk on or stand over a manhole lid.

Puzzle 4: Color the sketch and identify the hazard!!!

Answer: Back drive while removing vehicle from the garage or parking has become a very common cause of injury to children. Always make sure no child is present behind the car while removing it from parking. In the above picture you can see children playing behind the car. If the person removing car from the garage is not aware of these children, they may get hurt.

<u>Puzzle 5: Color the sketch and identify the hazard!!!</u>

Distracted driving has become another common cause of road traffic accidents. Always avoid multitasking when you are driving your vehicle.

As shown in the above picture, always follow traffic rules. Red light means stop, yellow means watch and drive carefully, while green means you can start driving.

Puzzle 6: Color the sketch and identify the hazard!!!

Roads are meant for faster transport. Vehicles move on the road at a fast pace and if we play on the road we may get injured because of these fast-moving vehicles. So never play on the road.

When we are sitting inside a car, every person should use seat belt. Seat belts protect our head from moving forward and getting injured at the time of accident.

Interesting facts:

SPEED	TIME TO GO 25KM	TIME SAVED	RISK OF ACCIDENT
80 km/hour	18 min	-	X
96 km/hour	16 min	02 min	2.0 X
112 km/hour	14 min	04 min	4.0 X
120 km/hour	13 min	Only 05 min	8.0 X

With the increase in the speed of the vehicle risk of accident increases by many folds but the time saved is very little. So never drive at higher speed. Little delay is always better than risk of accident.

Here is the list of some road signs that every person should know (Credits: https://mvd.kerala.gov.in/en/traffic-signs) ….

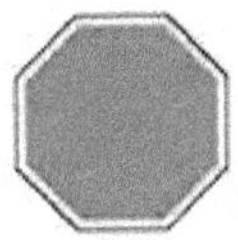

STOP

GIVE WAY

ONE WAY

NO ENTRY

ONE WAY

NO WAY
BOTH DIRECTION

RIGHT TURN
PROHIBITED

LEFT TURN
PROHIBITED

U-TURN
PROHIBITED

OVER TAKING
PROHIBITED

HORNS
PROHIBITED

SPEED
LIMIT

COMPULSORY
TURN LEFT

COMPULSORY
AHEAD ONLY

COMPULSORY
TURN RIGHT AHEAD

COMPULSORY AHEAD
OR TURN RIGHT

COMPULSORY AHEAD
OR TURN LEFT

COMPULSORY
KEEP LEFT

COMPULSORY
SOUND HORN

RIGHT HAND
CURVE

LEFT HAND
CURVE

RIGHT HAIR
PIN BEND

LEFT HAIR
PIN BEND

RIGHT REVERSE
BEND

LEFT REVERSE
BEND

STEEP
ASCENT

STEEP
DESCENT

NARROW
ROAD AHEAD

ROAD
WIDENS AHEAD

NARROW
BRIDGE

SLIPPERY
ROAD

LOOSE
GRAVEL

PEDESTRIAN
CROSSING

SCHOOL
AHEAD

MAN AT
WORK

CROSS
ROAD

GAP IN
MEDIAN

SIDE ROAD
RIGHT

SIDE ROAD
LEFT

Y - INTER
SECTION

Y - INTER
SECTION

Y - INTER
SECTION

T - INTER
SECTION

STAGGERED
INTERSECTION

STAGGERED
INTERSECTION

MAJOR ROAD
AHEAD

MAJOR ROAD
AHEAD

ROUND
ABOUT

DANGEROUS
DIP

HUMP OR
ROUGH ROAD

UNGUARDED
LEVEL CROSSING

GUARDED
LEVEL CROSSING

ACTIVITY: 19

Raj and his family were going on a family vacation by train. They were all excited to get on the train and start their trip.

Raj was standing on the platform, waiting for the train to arrive. He was so excited that he didn't notice how close he was standing to the tracks.

Suddenly, Scientia appeared.

"Raj, don't stand so close to the tracks!" Scientia said. "It's not safe."

"Why not?" Raj asked. "I'm just waiting for the train."

"Because the train could come at any time," Scientia said. "And if you're standing too close, you could get hit."

"But I'm careful," Raj said. "I'll jump out of the way if I see the train coming."

"You may be careful, but you might not be fast enough," Scientia said. "And it's not worth the risk."

Raj looked at the tracks, and he realized that Scientia was right. It wasn't safe to stand so close to the tracks. He didn't want to get hurt, so he moved away.

"Okay," Raj said. "I'll stand back."

Raj moved away from the tracks, and he waited for the train to arrive. He was grateful to Scientia for helping him to stay safe, and he knew that he would be more careful in the future.

The train arrived, and Raj and his family boarded. They had a wonderful time on their vacation, and they were all safe thanks to Scientia.

Here are some additional tips for staying safe around train tracks:

- **Always stand back from the edge of the platform when waiting for a train.**
- **Never cross the tracks unless you're sure the train is not coming.**
- **Never play on the tracks.**
- **If you see something on the tracks, tell a grown-up.**
- **Obey all train safety signs.**

<u>Maze Puzzle 1:</u>

Hazards:
Train

Safe zone

<u>Puzzle 2:</u>

An electric train is moving south at 120 mph speed and the flow of wind is towards the west at 20mph. Which way does the smoke from the train go?

Answer: Electric trains do not produce smoke.

Puzzle 3: Color the sketch and identify the hazard!!!

Can you spot the hazard in the above picture?

Answer: In the above picture a girl is standing too close to a railway track. Never stand too close to a railway track. A moving train causes a drop of pressure around it. This is called the Venturi effect. If you are standing too close to a moving train, you may get pushed towards the moving train because of reduced pressure and this may cause injury to you.

ACTIVITY: 20

Raj and his friends were playing in the park. They were having a lot of fun, and they were getting hungry.

Suddenly, a stranger approached them. He was carrying a bag of cookies, and he offered them to Raj and his friends.

The cookies looked delicious, and Raj was about to take one when Scientia appeared.

"Raj, don't take those cookies!" Scientia said. "They're not from a safe source."

"Why not?" Raj asked. "They look so good."

"Because you don't know who this person is," Scientia said. "They could be dangerous."

"But he seems nice," Raj said. "He offered us cookies."

"That doesn't mean he's safe," Scientia said. "There are a lot of people who will try to hurt children, and they'll often use candy or toys to lure them in. It's important to be careful around strangers, and to never take anything from them."

Raj looked at the cookies, and he realized that Scientia was right. He didn't know who this person was, and he didn't want to take any chances.

"Okay," Raj said. "I won't take the cookies."

The stranger looked disappointed, but he didn't say anything. He just turned and walked away.

Raj and his friends were grateful to Scientia for helping them to stay safe, and they knew that they would be more careful in the future.

"Thank you, Scientia," Raj said. "I'm glad you stopped me."

"You're welcome," Scientia said. "It's important to be careful around strangers."

Raj and his friends continued to play in the park, and they had a lot of fun. They were all safe thanks to Scientia, and they knew that they would be more careful in the future.

Here are some additional tips for staying safe around strangers:

- **Never take anything from a stranger.**
- **Never go anywhere with a stranger.**
- **If a stranger tries to talk to you, tell a grown-up.**
- **If you feel uncomfortable around a stranger, trust your gut and get away.**
- **Be aware of your surroundings and pay attention to who is around you.**
- **If you see something suspicious, tell a grown-up.**

Maze Puzzle 1:

Puzzle 2:

Do you know how pediatricians determine whether babies are growing normal or not?

Answer: Paediatricians look for various signs to access growth of babies. For example, when a baby is 2-month-old s/he can recognize parents, gives social smile, lifts shoulder when prone and coos. When a baby is 4-month-old s/he can laugh and squeal, roll front to back. When baby is 6-month-old s/he can sit unassisted, transfer objects hand to hand, feed self and hold bottle and develop **stranger anxiety.** If babies do not develop signs representative of a particular age paediatrician start searching for reason behind them.

Can you spot hazard in above picture?
Answer: In the above picture, one stranger is giving chocolate to a small girl. Never talk or take anything from strangers. Strangers with bad motives can hurt you.

ACTIVITY: 21

Raj and his friends were standing in a public place. They were waiting for their parents to pick them up.

A stranger was smoking nearby. He was blowing smoke in the air, and it was making Raj and his friends cough.

"Hey," Raj said to the stranger. "Can you please stop smoking? It's making us cough."

The stranger looked at Raj and his friends. He didn't say anything, but he took a drag on his cigarette and blew the smoke in their faces.

Raj and his friends were starting to get angry. They didn't know what to do.

Suddenly, Scientia appeared.

"Excuse me," Scientia said to the stranger. "Do you know that smoking is harmful to your health?"

The stranger looked at Scientia. He didn't say anything, but he took another drag on his cigarette.

"Smoking can cause cancer, heart disease, and lung disease," Scientia said. "It can also cause birth defects in babies. It's not only harmful to you, but it's also harmful to others. When you smoke in public, you're exposing people to secondhand smoke, which can also be harmful."

The stranger looked at Scientia for a moment. He then put out his cigarette and threw it on the ground.

"Sorry," he said. "I didn't know."

"It's okay," Scientia said. "Just remember to be more mindful of others in the future."

The stranger nodded. He then walked away.

Raj and his friends were grateful to Scientia for helping them. They knew that she was right, and they would be more careful in the future.

"Thank you, Scientia," Raj said. "You saved us from secondhand smoke."

"You're welcome," Scientia said. "It's important to be aware of the dangers of smoking."

Raj and his friends continued to wait for their parents to pick them up. They were all safe thanks to Scientia, and they knew that they would be more careful in the future.

Maze Puzzle 1:

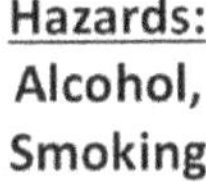

<u>Puzzle 2: Identify the hazard!!!</u>

Smoking cigarettes or drinking alcohol is injurious to our health. Smoke from cigarettes affects not only the person who is using it but also the people standing near it. This smoke is highly dangerous and can affect our lungs and cause deadly diseases like cancer. Just like cigarettes, alcohol is also dangerous. Alcohol makes people lazy and irresponsible. Alcohol causes diseases like obesity, diabetes, hypertension, liver failure, liver cancer etc. Alcohol makes people irresponsible towards their family, work, health and society.

Puzzle 3: Color the sketch and identify the hazard!!!

Adults should never sleep with small baby beside them. During sleep adult may roll over baby and cause injury to baby. In fact, this is a very common cause of injury to babies. Always use small separator between adult and baby to avoid this.

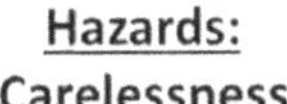

Hazards:
Carelessness

Safe zone

Educate your family and friends about these safety tips

Baby safety tips:

1. Sleep on back.
2. Children younger than 2 years should sleep in cribs.
3. Never keep any pillow or stuffed animal in baby crib.
4. Avoid nuts, carrots, popcorn, coconut pieces.
5. Keep coin, batteries, small toys, magnets, and toy parts away from children.